THE HAUNTED TOWER

Susannah Leigh

Illustrated by Brenda Haw

Designed by Brian Robertson
and Kim Blundell

Cover design: Michelle Lawrence

Edited by Karen Dolby

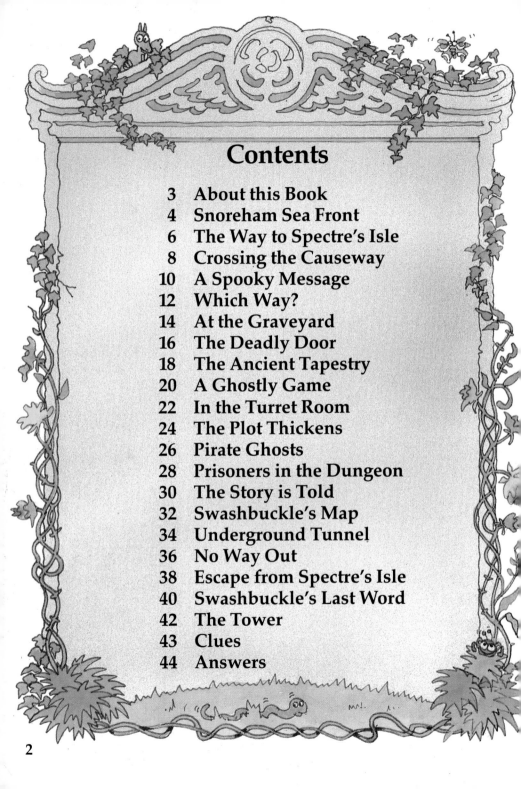

Contents

3　About this Book
4　Snoreham Sea Front
6　The Way to Spectre's Isle
8　Crossing the Causeway
10　A Spooky Message
12　Which Way?
14　At the Graveyard
16　The Deadly Door
18　The Ancient Tapestry
20　A Ghostly Game
22　In the Turret Room
24　The Plot Thickens
26　Pirate Ghosts
28　Prisoners in the Dungeon
30　The Story is Told
32　Swashbuckle's Map
34　Underground Tunnel
36　No Way Out
38　Escape from Spectre's Isle
40　Swashbuckle's Last Word
42　The Tower
43　Clues
44　Answers

About this Book

The Haunted Tower is a spooky adventure story with a difference. The difference is that you can take part in the adventure.

Throughout the book, there are lots of ghostly puzzles and perplexing problems which you must solve in order to understand the next part of the story.

Look at the pictures carefully and watch out for vital clues. Sometimes you will need to flick back through the book to help you find an answer. There are extra clues on page 43 and you can check the answers on pages 44 to 48.

Just turn the page to begin the adventure . . .

Charlie

Ali

Nic

Nic and Ali are visiting their cousin Charlie at the seaside town of Port Snoreham for the first time.

Snoreham Sea Front

Charlie, Nic and Ali were busy slurping ice creams on the first afternoon of their vacation in Port Snoreham. Ali pointed at a dark, wooded island on which stood a tall, mysterious tower. She wondered what it was called.

"That's Spectre's Isle," said Charlie. "They say the tower's haunted by a ghostly pirate called Captain Swashbuckle. He built the tower hundreds of years ago and there he planned his daring sea voyages.

Then, one stormy night, his ship hit a reef off the island and sank without trace. The legend says an incredible hoard of treasure was lost with Swashbuckle and his crew, but it has never been found. Now Swashbuckle's ghost is said to haunt the tower."

Nic peered through the beach telescope for a closer look and gasped in amazement, scarcely believing her eyes. Could the legend be true?

5

The Way to Spectre's Isle

Was the tower haunted? Nic and Ali could hardly wait to investigate. But first they had to find a way to Spectre's Isle.

"No one ever dares go there," Charlie said, nervously. "Besides, it's impossible ."

Ali asked some townspeople and was told there was a causeway across to the island, but it was usually flooded. The rest of the information was very puzzling.

But when Charlie checked the tides and Nic looked at her diary, they realized they could reach the island at a certain time of the day.

When can they cross the causeway?

JUNE
MON 17 D
Ali's birthday.
TUES 18 Sports day.
Egg + spoon race –
remember egg.
WED 19 I owe John
3 gobstoppers.
THURS 20
Tiggy to vets.

FRI 21 ○
Snoreham holiday
begins. Meet Charlie 4 p.m.
SAT 22
Mum's birthday.
SUN 23
Buy Kite.
NOTES French homework
for Msr. Garlique

GREAT SNOREHAM TIDE TIMES
For neighbouring towns + or – minutes
as shown:

+ 49 – GREAT GRUNGEBY
+ 07 – SLIMEBAG BAY
– 12 – PORT SNOREHAM
– 26 – BILGE WATERS

JUNE	HIGH	LOW
20	05.18, 17.42	11.27, 23.40
21	05.54, 18.15	12.04
22	06.28, 18.46	00.12, 12.35
23	06.57, 19.14	01.10, 13.30
24	07.52, 20.06	01.36, 13.54

Bream's baskets

Crossing the Causeway

That night, just as the numbers on Charlie's extra-tough-all-weather-underwater-survival watch changed to 00.00 hours, they arrived at the causeway.

"We're almost there," said Nic, pointing at the tower, ahead.

"Hang on," Charlie shivered. "I don't like the look of those spiky rocks or the quicksand."

Ali agreed, "And watch out for the crabs and octopusses."

"And those starfish look dangerous," gulped Charlie. "I wonder if the jellyfish are poisonous?"

"Follow me," said Nic, sounding braver than she felt.

Can you find a safe route across the causeway? Be careful!

DOGFISH

9

A Spooky Message

Damp and bedraggled, they stepped ashore into a dark forest. Tall trees closed in on all sides and moonlight shone through the branches, making sinister patterns on the ground.

Through the trees, they could just see the top of the tower, shadowy and mysterious in the darkness. Slowly, they crept toward it. Charlie heard a strange, ghostly echo. Ali had a feeling they were being watched. It was very spooky.

At last they saw the tower in front of them. At the same time, two shimmering forms appeared floating in midair.

"Ghosts!" gasped Charlie, terrified by their staring white faces and glinting cutlasses.

While the trio stared in horror, the ghostly apparitions glided slowly away around the side of the tower. As they went, a small piece of paper fluttered to the ground. Feeling a bit shaky, Nic picked it up and stared at the meaningless list of words.

"What is it?" puzzled Ali, peering at the note.

"Perhaps it's a ghostly code," exclaimed Charlie, trying to work out what it meant.

What does the strange note say?

4·30 FRIDAY. KK FROM FF TO BB. AND TO GO GRAVEYARD THE FOR TONIGHT INFORMATION FURTHER YOU ABOUT WHO. KNOW MEET THEN IN ME TOWER THE THE AT HOUR. WITCHING TAKE YOU FLOATING THE AND PHANTOM, TO REMEMBER IT HIDE YOU WHEN THERE. GET GHOULS PS GHOSTS AND AND AWAKE THE LET BEGIN. HAUNTING MAY WE GUESTS HAVE TONIGHT.

Which Way?

Phantoms, ghouls, ghosts . . . what did it mean? And what about "you know who"? Nic was determined to find the answers and that meant going to the graveyard.

"I don't like the idea of seeing those ghosts again," Charlie gulped.

"Besides," Ali pointed out. "We don't know the way. These woods are so dark we could be wandering for ever."

But Nic had made up her mind and marched along the only path leading from the tower. Ali and Charlie had to run to keep up. Soon they came to a clearing with mysterious, overgrown paths branching off in all directions. An old, rotten signpost lay on the ground.

Looking closely at the bits, Nic thought for a moment. With a flash of inspiration, she realized they could still use the sign to find the path to the graveyard.

Which path leads to the graveyard?

At the Graveyard

At the end of the path, a chilling mist began swirling around them. Through it, they could see the tall iron gates of the graveyard and the ancient stones beyond. The shadows of the tombs lengthened eerily in the flashlight beam and even Nic wondered if they should go in.

Charlie hung nervously behind, while Ali and Nic ventured inside the gates. Immediately Ali spotted something odd. Lying on the ground was a large sheet of paper.

"How strange," said Ali, puzzled. "It's got holes cut in it."

14

Nic looked at the paper and realized it was exactly the same size as some of the gravestones. This gave her an idea. She was sure she was right.

"This paper is more valuable than you think," she exclaimed. "It's the key to a message."

Can you read the message?

The Deadly Door

They looked at each other in horror. Who could the prisoner be and why was he doomed to die? Could they save him, or were they already too late? The only way to find out was to return to the tower.

They raced back through the woods and tiptoed around the tower looking for a way in.

"Over here," Ali hissed to the other two. "We can get in this way."

Charlie wasn't too pleased at this. He would have liked an excuse to turn around and leave. Even Nic's teeth were chattering as they tiptoed up the steps and under the portcullis. Would they see the ghosts again?

Inside the coast was clear, but getting into the rest of the tower was not going to be so easy. Facing them was a solid wooden door, bolted and barred by a heavy beam. They tried hard, but could not move it.

It was then they noticed a lever attached to a cog mechanism. It seemed to be an elaborate lock and the only way of opening the door. Charlie ran up the short flight of stone steps and grasped the lever.

"Watch out!" called Ali. "If you turn the handle the wrong way that enormous spiky cannon ball will fall on you!"

Which way must Charlie turn the handle?

The Ancient Tapestry

Inside the door was a winding stone staircase. Slowly the trio made their way up. At the top an old door creaked as Nic pushed against it. The three peered in to see suits of armor, glinting in the darkness.

They crept into the dimly-lit room. It looked as if no one had been in there for years. Then Charlie spotted an old piece of cloth tucked between a suit of armor and the wall. It looked interesting.

He tugged hard. With a great RIP the material came away from its hiding place. At that moment, there was a loud rumbling sound and the whole ceiling began to give way. They dashed out of the room just in time.

Charlie looked at the material as it fell to pieces. It was a tapestry. The pictures were torn and muddled, but bit by bit he was able to read the story.

What does the tapestry say?

TOWER LEADS A LIFE OF ADVENTURE ON THE HIGH SEAS AND

HIS PRECIOUS HOARD FROM PRYING EYES AND

to Captain Swashbuckle, in April 1741.

TREASURE AND PRICELESS JEWELS, MORTALLY

SEPTIMUS SWASHBUCKLE, CAPTAIN OF THE PEPPERY

A Ghostly Game

So the old legend was wrong. Swashbuckle's treasure wasn't at the bottom of the sea after all. It seemed to be hidden somewhere in the tower. But where was it? In front of them, in the dust-filled corridor, was an open door. Were there more clues inside?

Quickly they slipped into the room. The door clicked tightly shut behind them. A strange, yellow light flickered all around and in the shadows they could see furniture, a small spiral staircase and...

"Ghosts!" gasped Charlie.

I'll search the armor room and take a look downstairs. You two go upstairs and scour the turret and battlements.

No, Brian. You look in here. Katy and I will search the rest of this floor and check downstairs.

Codswallop, Fred. We'll look around here. Brian can search the turret and battlements.

Three shadowy figures sat huddled around a large table in the middle of the room. They were surrounded by bottles and candles and were whispering fiercely to one another.

The door had locked. There was no choice but to hide and hope the ghosts didn't notice them. Hardly daring to breathe and with knees knocking, they listened to the spooky voices.

After what seemed like hours, the ghoulish conversation ended. The ghostly figures slowly stood up, about to begin their mysterious search. Nic breathed a sigh of relief. She knew what to do now.

"Don't panic," she whispered. "I know where we can go to get away from those ghouls."

Which pirate has the highest score?
Which part of the tower is safe?

In the Turret Room

Lend us a fiver.

Before the ghosts turned round, Nic, Charlie and Ali dashed up the spiral stairs to the turret room. It looked as if it had not been disturbed for centuries. As their eyes got used to the dark, they realized this wasn't true. Then Ali spotted something which proved someone else had been in the room VERY recently.

What has Ali spotted?
What other odd things are there?

23

The Plot Thickens

HISTORIAN VANISHES

by Will E. Tell

Lord R. Kive

Swashbuckle's Hoard

Legend tells of Swashbuckle's fantastic hoard of priceless treasure. It was thought the hoard sank with Swashbuckle and his ship, but when Kive's team of divers recovered the wreck, no treasure was found.

POLICE ARE INVESTIGATING the mysterious disappearance of Lord Reggie Kive from his Port Snoreham home on Monday evening. Lord Kive is a well known historian and expert on Snoreham.

Kive made his most exciting discovery only weeks ago when he uncovered the long lost wreck of "The Peppery Cat", a 17th century pirate ship. It was owned by the notorious Captain Septimus Swashbuckle whose ghost is supposed to haunt the tower on Spectre's Isle.

No Clues

Rumor has it that Kive was on the point of discovering the secret of Swashbuckle's treasure when he vanished without trace. Police are treating his disappearance as suspicious, but as yet have no firm leads.

Mystery

Lord Kive's housekeeper, Mrs Kleenupp, said when interviewed yesterday, "Larks-a-mercy dearies, it's not like him to go off without saying anything. He always leaves a note. Something terrible must have happened . . ."

HORROR SCOPE

Predicted for you by Ann Dromeda.

AQUARIUS
The full moon could bring some changes to your life.

PISCES
Beware of new events. Something fishy is going on.

ARIES
It's a good time to move house. You have been feeling restless.

TAURUS
Take the bull by the horns and explore undiscovered territory.

GEMINI
Your fear of the unknown will grow greater this month.

CANCER
Don't let unexplained events put you off exploring new horizons.

LEO
You will meet a tall, dark, shadowy figure.

VIRGO
People from the past may well be on your mind.

LIBRA
Lately, you have been feeling like a different person.

SCORPIO
You will soon be making a journey across water.

SAGITTARIUS
A well-kept secret will be revealed to you.

CAPRICORN
Even your best laid plans will go astray.

WEATHER FORECAST
Coastal areas will experience sunshine and warmer weather, but offshore islands will suffer thunder storms and occasional lightning flashes.

Charlie reached up and grabbed the newspaper. It fell open at the middle pages and a familiar name caught his eye.

Swashbuckle! He began reading the story when suddenly he noticed something interesting about the crossword.

SNOREHAM NEWS, 21st JUNE

CROSSWORD CLUES

ACROSS

1 Season between Spring and Autumn.
3 Scurrying creatures. Like mice, but larger.
(5) Relates to the time before noon and p.m.
(7) Caught without means of escape.
10 "For _____ and _____. Amen." What word is missing?
12 Close fitting short coat of soldier or policeman.
(13) Myself.
15 Word that is used for a male.
(17) "The Wind _____ _____ Willows." What words are missing? (2 letters. 3 letters.)
18 Sound of a bell.
(21) Underground cell. Place for a fantasy game with a dragon!
22 Mum and Dad are sometimes called Ma and _____ ?
24 Not at all fast.

(25) Polite word to use when asking for something.

DOWN

1 Large area of salt water.
2 A rebellion where men refuse to obey officers.
3 Stout cord that might be used as a lasso.
4 Rise and fall of the sea.
6 Good friend.
(8) Place in which information or records are stored.
9 Adam's partner in the Garden of Eden.
11 Small kind of deer.
13 What kind of maid is half-woman and half-fish?
(14) Right away. Immediately. (2 letters. 4 letters)
(15) Assist. Lend a hand.
16 Kind of antelope.
19 Sacred image or statue.
20 Wear away by biting.
23 She drank her cocoa and _____ her supper.

TOP 5 BESTSELLING BOOKS

1. Danger at Demon's Cove.
2. The Intergalactic Bus Trip.
3. Curse of the Lost Idol.
4. The Incredible Dinosaur Expedition.
5. The Haunted Tower.

CLASSIFIED ADS

EMBARRASSING BALDNESS? Premature aging? Old before your time? Come to Dr Grizzly's health farm for a complete recovery program.

WANTED: New roof for house in Greenwhat. Tel.540 0525.

PROFESSIONAL Company seeks new offices. Any offers considered. Tel.379 999

LOSE WEIGHT fast the Bilge Waters way!

PASS first time! Easy-drive with the Chiang-Choong School of Motoring. Tel.765 8090

COMING SOON – to a theater near you! The Amazing Adventures of Agent Arthur – a new kind of Super Hero.

EAT at Katy Krayfish's Kozy Koffee Korner, for the best cakes in Snoreham. On the seafront.

SUZY'S COCKTAILS Mango Miracle a speciality.

FOR SALE: Tower, one previous owner, deceptively spacious. In need of some attention. Oliver Skint Estate Agents.

Some of the clues had been ringed with black ink. It seemed very odd. Quickly he set about solving them.

At last things began to click into place.

What has Charlie worked out?

Pirate Ghosts

The vanishing historian, Lord R. Kive was the prisoner in the tower! His plea for help sounded desperate. There was still a chance they could save him if they moved fast. Charlie led the way to the dungeon. But halfway down, Nic realized they were not alone. A large, mean-looking pirate was hot on their trail.

Charlie hurtled toward the bottom step. Before he could stop himself, he crashed BANG into a surprisingly solid pirate ghost, standing at the foot of the stairs. At that moment, another ghastly spectre appeared. Nic, Charlie and Ali were surrounded with no hope of escape.

There was silence for one terrible minute. Ali looked at the pirates more closely. She realized these "ghosts" were very human. In fact, she even knew their names.

"You made a big mistake meddling with us," sneered one of the pirates, picking himself up. "Now we have no choice but to imprison you here . . . for ever."

"Yes," sniggered the woman, marching them off. "It's down to the dungeon with you three."

Who are the pirate "ghosts"?

26

Prisoners in the Dungeon

BANG. The door was slammed shut and locked firmly behind them. Charlie heard Fred Fillet's evil cackles floating down the corridor.

"Hah, hah, hah. I hope you enjoy your final anchoring place, me hearties," he chortled.

Was this the end for them all? Were they to be left for ever in the dark and dreary dungeon, doomed to die?

Suddenly, from out of the shadows shuffled a small, dishevelled-looking figure. He stepped into the light and they gasped in amazement. He could only be...

"Lord Kive," exclaimed Charlie.

"Pleased to meet you," said Kive. "So I WAS right. I knew there was someone else in the tower."

He explained that the foul fiends, Bream, Fillet and Krayfish had kidnapped him and brought him to the tower. He hid his plea for help in the crossword and managed to leave the newspaper in the turret room when he was taken there for interrogation.

"But why did they kidnap you?" asked Ali.

"I'll explain later, m'dear," he said. "First, we must escape."

There was a small, open window, but it was impossible to reach even standing on each others' shoulders. Ali sat down miserably on the damp, sandy floor and without thinking, built a castle.

"How can you play silly games at a time like this?" Nic started to say, when a brilliant escape plan began to form in her head.

What is Nic's escape plan?

The Story is Told

Nic and Ali helped Lord Kive to his feet after he had scrambled through the bushes.

"Phew, that was a hefty climb," he wheezed.

"But I think you'll agree it was a clever idea, sir," Nic boasted.

"Indeed it was m'dear. But there's no time to lose. Those crooks will soon realize we've gone and then there'll be trouble."

Ali was still puzzled. She wanted to know what was going on. What were Fillet and his fishy crew up to? And why had Kive been held prisoner in the tower? As they brushed themselves down, Kive began to tell them his story.

After months searching, I discovered where the wreck of Swashbuckle's ship was lying. I was sure the treasure did exist and sent down divers to explore.

No treasure was found, but the diving team returned with a sealed casket, filled with Swashbuckle's papers. Among them was a map of Spectre's Isle.

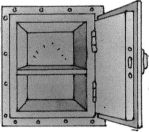

The map belonged to Swashbuckle and it seemed to pinpoint the whereabouts of his treasure.

That night, there was a burglary at my house. Fillet and his two cronies stole the old map.

But the clues on it are fiendishly difficult and the thieves couldn't work them out.

Knowing my reputation for code breaking, the villains returned. They blindfolded and kidnapped me and brought me, a prisoner, to the tower.

They threatened me and tried to force me to help them in their ruthless quest for the treasure. But I have managed to resist their demands.

31

Swashbuckle's Map

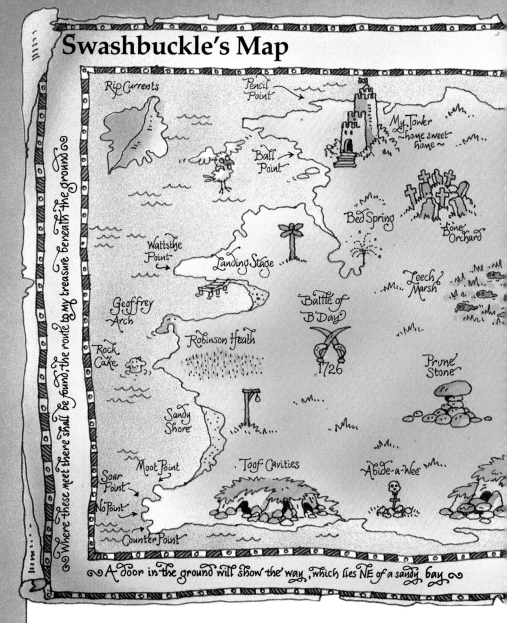

Rip Currents

Pencil Point

My Tower
~home sweet home~

Ball Point

Bed Spring

Bone Orchard

Wattsthe Point

Landing Stage

Leech Marsh

Geoffrey Arch

Battle of B Day

Rock Cake

Robinson Heath

1726

Prune Stone

Sandy Shore

Moot Point

Toof Cavities

Abide-a-Wee

Soar Point

No Point

Counter Point

Where these meet there shall be found, the route to my treasure beneath the ground

A door in the ground will show the way, which lies NE of a sandy bay

All of a sudden Charlie remembered the tapestry he had found.

"It seems to say the treasure's hidden in the tower," he said.

"Then my map should lead us to it," Lord Kive said, excitedly. "I have it safe here in my pocket. Those vile villains gave it back to me so that I could decipher the clues for them."

My secret lies beneath a tree, Small and twisty as ye shall see

Pointer Point

Ficker Woods

Bennee Hill

Sticky End Swamp

Door Creek

Marsh Mallow

Fick Woods

Severd Head

Norty Buoy

N

Battle of Garrick

Konn Caves

1732

Lifesa Beach

Sticking Point

Door Quay

NNW of a battle ground, NE of a marsh and N of a mound

— This map belongs to Captain Septimus Swashbuckle —

There wasn't a moment to lose. Fillet and his friends were bound to discover their escape soon and give chase. They studied the map carefully. At first the clues didn't make sense.

Then Charlie realized they were muddled up and began putting them in order.

What do the clues say?
Where do they lead?

Underground Tunnel

They followed the clues to the small, twisted tree and began clearing away the fallen leaves and earth, in search of the trapdoor.

"Here it is," Nic cried, digging up a rusty handle.

She had found the ancient door. It was stiff with age, but they managed to lever it open. Soon they were staring into the dark depths of an underground passage. Warily they stepped in. Their way was lit by the moon shining eerily into the long, winding tunnel.

The path twisted and turned, and the stony ground was hard to walk on. Charlie jumped as something small and furry scuttled across his foot. At long last, the path began to slope steeply upwards and they saw a chink of light shining above them. Scrambling up some stone steps towards it, they found themselves in a small, cold room.

When their eyes adjusted to the dim light they glanced around the room and gasped in amazement. Dusty portraits lined the walls. Charlie thought some of the pictures looked familiar but he couldn't be sure.

Just then Kive spotted a gleam of light coming from a small alcove. He reached in and pulled out . . .

. . . a magnificent golden cup encrusted with jewels. Surely this was Swashbuckle's treasure. Lord Kive could hardly believe his eyes. Nic, Charlie and Ali clustered round for a better look.

"Swashbuckle's long-lost chalice," Kive gasped, carefully examining it. "This is legendary. A priceless historical find . . . and I'm holding it."

No Way Out

Lord Kive beamed with delight as he gazed at the chalice.

"I can never thank you enough for helping me find it," he said.

Nic looked glum. After all their detective work, this didn't seem much like real treasure. She had expected a great hoard of pirate gold, doubloons and pieces of eight. But there was no time to feel disappointed.

"Sshhh," Ali hissed. "There's someone coming this way."

All four listened and heard the unmistakeable voices of Fillet and his friends echoing up from the depths of the tunnel. Before long, they would be here.

In desperation, they searched for another way out, but there was only the tunnel. They were trapped. Then something in one of the paintings caught Ali's eye.

"There's a secret door," she cried. "And I know where it is."

Where is the secret door?
How do they open it?

Escape from Spectre's Isle

They stepped straight out into the entrance hall.

"That was a narrow escape," said Ali. "But we're safe now."

Just then the door creaked open and Fillet's foot appeared. The gang were right behind them.

Nic took charge as the fishy felons burst through the secret door. There was only one thing they could do.

"Run for it!" she yelled.

The others sprinted after her and dashed out of the tower.

They raced down the hill heading for the shore. Charlie glanced back over his shoulder and gulped. The criminals were still hard on their heels, getting closer every second.

Then Charlie had a brainwave. He kicked a small, round stone towards the pursuing villains. Bream stepped on it and went flying, closely followed by his crooked cronies.

While the fake ghosts untangled themselves, Charlie, Nic, Ali and Kive stumbled down the rough path to the sea front. But when they got there, they looked around in horror. The causeway was under water. Ali spotted a small rubber dinghy, but it was only big enough for one. They were trapped!

The situation was desperate. Nic's brain clunked into gear. She thought back to the ghostly coded message and realized there MUST be another means of escape, if only they could find it.

How can they escape from Spectre's Isle?

Swashbuckle's Last Word

Charlie and Ali quickly dragged the boat across the rocks and lowered it into the sea.

"Let's go," shouted Kive, grabbing the oars.

The villains raced across the beach towards them. Ali waded into the water, pushing the boat out into the shallows.

"Jump aboard," yelled Charlie. "I can fix that creepy crew."

In one swift movement he grabbed a pirate cutlass from the bottom of the boat and plunged it into the rubber dinghy. Ali leapt into the boat as Nic and Kive rowed with all their might away from the shore. The crooks were left floundering behind.

The boat bobbed up and down on the choppy sea. Ali examined the chalice for the first time and found the lid lifted off easily. She peered inside and was amazed to discover a piece of parchment. It was obviously a message from Swashbuckle, but most of it was written in a very strange way. Slowly it began to make sense, except for one thing . . . where was the ruby ring?

What does the message say? Where is the ruby ring?

I Septimus Swashbuckle am dying of wounds sustained in bloody battle and shall never live to enjoy the treasures I have won.

S. Swashbuckle 1 May 1741

The Tower

Back at Snoreham, everything happened very quickly. A police boat sped off to pick up the crooks, still on the island.

"Imagine those thugs thinking they could scare us by dressing up and pretending to be pirate ghosts," Charlie scoffed.

With Lord Kive and the chalice safe at the museum, the trio walked along the seafront. They couldn't believe they had found the first clue in Swashbuckle's treasure trail.

As they planned their tropical treasure hunt, Nic looked at the island through the beach binoculars. She could just see Fillet, Bream and Krayfish leaping up and down on the shore.

"Something seems to have frightened them," she said.

Peering closely at the island, the tower looked as dark and mysterious as ever. At once, she saw what had scared the gang.

What has Nic seen?

Clues

Pages 6-7

Look carefully at all the information. What day is it?

Pages 8-9

This is easy. They can jump from rock to rock and use the anchor as a bridge.

Pages 10-11

Try swapping the first word with the second word. Keep going.

Pages 12-13

If the signpost was standing, the sign to the tower would point to the path they have just walked down.

Pages 14-15

Trace the piece of paper and place it over each of the gravestones in turn. Look at the words that appear through the holes.

Pages 16-17

If one cog turns clockwise, the next cog will turn anticlockwise, unless they are connected by a straight rubber band.

Pages 18-19

Trace the tapestry and fit the pieces together. The pictures and words tell a story.

Pages 20-21

Who wins the game of dice? Brian scores 4 with his first throw.

Pages 22-23

This is easy. Use your eyes.

Pages 24-25

Solve the ringed crossword clues. The answers can be rearranged to form a message.

Pages 26-27

Look closely at the people on the Snoreham sea front.

Pages 28-29

This is easier than it looks. Sand is the clue.

Pages 32-33

Try putting the clues in order, using the rhymes as a guideline. Then follow the compass directions carefully.

Pages 36-37

Look closely at everything in the room.

Pages 38-39

Think back to the ghostly message on page 11.

Pages 40-41

Look carefully at the chalice and at Swashbuckle's portrait.

Page 42

Can you see anything strange on the island?

Answers

Pages 6-7

They can cross the causeway at midnight (00.00 hours) tonight.

This is how they work it out:
They are told that they can only cross at low tide and when the moon is full. The date is June 21st, the first day of their Snoreham holiday. Nic's diary shows that they will meet Charlie at 4 p.m. and says there is a full moon that night. According to the tidetable the next low tide is at 00.12 hrs on June 22nd, at Great Snoreham. Low tide at Port Snoreham is 12 minutes earlier. This means that the next low tide is at 00.00 hrs, or midnight.

Pages 8-9

The route across the causeway is marked in black.

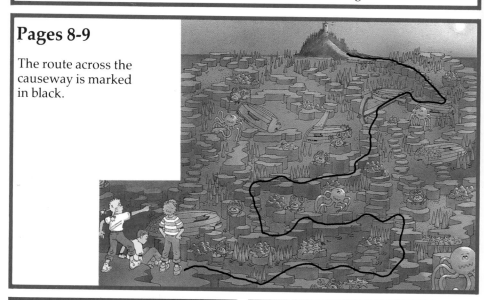

Pages 10-11

The message is decoded by swapping the first word with the next, and so on. This is what it says:

Friday 4.30. From KK to FF and BB. Go to the graveyard for further information about you know who. Then meet me in the tower at the witching hour. You take the Floating Phantom, and remember to hide it when you get there. PS Ghouls and ghosts awake and let the haunting begin. We may have guests tonight.

Pages 12-13

This is what the signpost would look like if the pieces were fitted together.

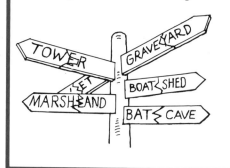

They can find the path to the graveyard by fitting together the pieces of the signpost and standing it up so the tower sign points to the path leading to the tower. All the other signs will then point in the correct directions.

This path leads to the graveyard.

Pages 14-15

When the paper is placed over this gravestone, these words appear through the holes:

TOWER PRISONER WILL DIE SOON.

Pages 16-17

The wheel must be turned anticlockwise to open the door. The arrows show the direction in which each cog turns.

Pages 18-19

SEPTIMUS SWASHBUCKLE, CAPTAIN OF THE PEPPERY CAT, COMMANDER OF A BRAVE BAND OF BUCCANEERS AND BUILDER OF THE TOWER LEADS A LIFE OF ADVENTURE ON THE HIGH SEAS AND AMASSES A HOARD OF

TREASURE AND PRICELESS JEWELS. MORTALLY WOUNDED IN BATTLE HE RETURNS TO HIS TOWER TO DIE AND HERE, HE PLANS TO HIDE HIS PRECIOUS HOARD FROM PRYING EYES AND GREEDY HANDS x x x x x x

hand sewn by Mrs Huggins, loyal tower-keeper to Captain Swashbuckle, in April 1761.

Pages 20-21

Fred has the highest score. The only possible scores that produce one winner are shown in the table. This means that the ghosts will adopt Fred's strategy. Only the turret room and battlements are safe.

	First throw	Second throw	Total
Brian	4	2	6
Katy	2	4	6
Fred	1	6	7

Pages 22-23

Ali has spotted a copy of the Snoreham News dated June 21st. This proves someone was in the room the previous day. There are several other modern things. These are ringed.

Pages 24-25

Charlie has worked out that the answers to the ringed clues can be rearranged to form this message:

AM TRAPPED IN THE DUNGEON. PLEASE HELP ME AT ONCE, ARCHIVE.

Here is the completed crossword. The answers to the ringed clues are shaded in grey.

SUMMER RATS
SE U O I
AM TRAPPED ED
A IR EVER
TUNIC E O
ME Y HA HE
E G INTHE
RING V OL
DUNGEON PA
O A C T
SLOW PLEASE

46

Pages 26-27

The imposters are the icecream seller on page 4, the basket maker and the coffee shop waitress, both on page 7. They are called Fred Fillet, Bosun Brian Bream and Katy Krayfish.

Pages 28-29

Nic's plan is to build a mound of sand against the wall, underneath the window. They can then climb up the mound and escape through the window.

Pages 32-33

When the clues are rearranged they form a rhyme:

My secret lies beneath a tree,
Small and twisty as ye shall see.
A door in the ground will show the way,

Which lies NE of a sandy bay.
NNW of a battleground,
NE of a marsh and W of a mound.
Where these points meet there shall be found,
The route to my treasure beneath the ground.

Draw a line from each of the places mentioned, in the compass direction specified. The point where the four lines cross marks the site of the small twisty tree. Underneath this spot is the trapdoor entrance to the secret tunnel leading to the treasure.

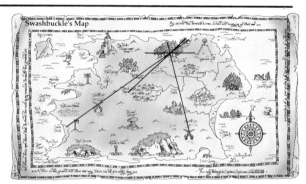

Pages 36-37

You can see a plan of the room in the background of Swashbuckle's portrait. A secret door is marked on it.

The secret door is here.

The rhyme in this book explains how to open the door. This is what it says:

A BUCKLE ON MY SECRET DOOR YOU'LL SEE
PRESS IT HARD AND YOU'LL BE FREE.

Pages 38-39

The message on page 11 mentions the Floating Phantom which is the boat Fred Fillet and Bosun Bream used to cross the island.

The boat is hidden here.
They can use it to escape.

Pages 40-41

Part of Swashbuckle's message is written backwards. It says:

My precious hoard lies far from here
Buried in sand by waters clear,
On a tropical island shaped like a bell,
There you must search and all will be well.
For here it is hidden, from here it's retrieved
And not from my tower as most have believed.
If my treasure you seek for unselfish ends
Good luck will befall you, you'll find it my friends.

As long as my ruby ring you possess
Success will be with you during your quest.
Beware and be warned all who start off without it,
My ghost shall haunt ye, forever, don't doubt it.

Here is the ring.

You can see Swashbuckle wearing the ring in the portrait on page 37.

Page 42

Nic has seen a strange white figure . . . the ghost of Captain Swashbuckle?

This edition first published in 2007 by Usborne Publishing Ltd., Usborne House, 83-85 Saffron Hill, London EC1N 8RT, England. www.usborne.com Copyright © 2007, 2001, 1989 Usborne Publishing Ltd.